UNWRINKLING
PLAYS

UNWRINKLING PLAYS

by paul reps

CHARLES E. TUTTLE COMPANY
Rutland, Vermont & Tokyo, Japan

Representatives

For Continental Europe:
BOXERBOOKS, INC., Zurich

For the British Isles:
PRENTICE-HALL INTERNATIONAL, INC., London

For Australasia:
PAUL FLESCH & CO., PTY. LTD., Melbourne

For Canada:
M. G. HURTIG LTD., Edmonton

Published by the Charles E. Tuttle Co., Inc.
of Rutland, Vermont and Tokyo, Japan
with editorial offices at
Suido 1-chome, 2-6, Bunkyo-ku, Tokyo, Japan

Copyright in Japan, 1965
by Charles E. Tuttle Co., Inc.

Library of Congress Catalog Card No. 65–12270

International Standard Book No. 0-8048-0607-1

First edition, 1965
Fourth printing, 1971

Book design and typography by Keiko Chiba
Printed in Japan

CONTENTS

Preface   7

20 PLAYS

operation   8
door   11
unwrinkling   14

seed   16
the big welling   19
turn   22

great waves, small waves   25
villagers   26
goat life   28

upstreaming   30
less than more   33
as if   37

the unkill   40
schoolroom   42
poison   44

dancing keys   46
boxed   48
attack   50
unknot   52
accordingly   55

Poem Show   59

PREFACE

The plays?

Whatever happens plays us.
These are produced (seen—heard—moved)
in you, me. This makes them "plays"
in the playful sense on the breezy
flaming real-life mind stage of attention.
Attention is the miracle.

The poems?

Something we see or hear poems us.
We feel it, free it, it frees us.
Incredible joy. Before why.

reps

OPERATION

A Doctor's Office.
Woman radiantly healthy enters with her sick self
moving in consonance with her.
WOMAN: This doesn't smell like a doctor's office.
THIN MAN *(enters led by his sick self):* I seem to have been
led here.

Nurse enters with her sick self.
The nurse, woman, and sick man do not notice their sick
selves.
NURSE: The doctor will see you soon.

Doctor enters.
The three sick selves hurriedly pick up medicines, drugs,
pills, surgical instruments, giving them to the doctor,
urging him to treat their well selves. He does so.
WOMAN *(with an appealing glance at the thin man):*
I only wanted to use the ladies' room.
THIN MAN *(as medicine is forced on him):* I am looking for
a plumber.
NURSE: The doctor will see you soon.
DOCTOR: Go home and rest. Everything will be all
right.

The three sick selves push the doctor to a couch, forcing
medicines on him. Assisted by the nurse, they begin to
operate.
DOCTOR *(just before the incision):* There's nothing wrong
with me!

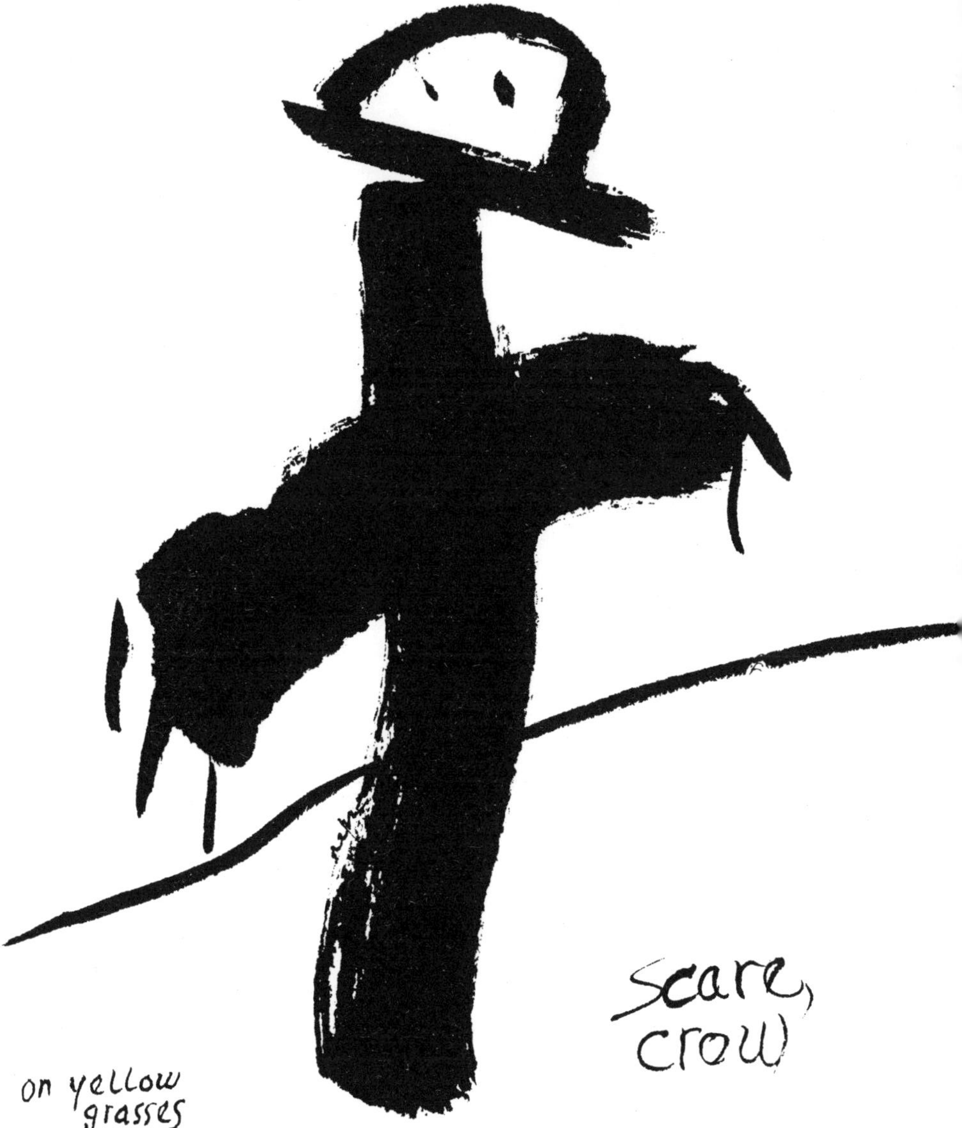

scare,
crow

on yellow
grasses
a day
passes

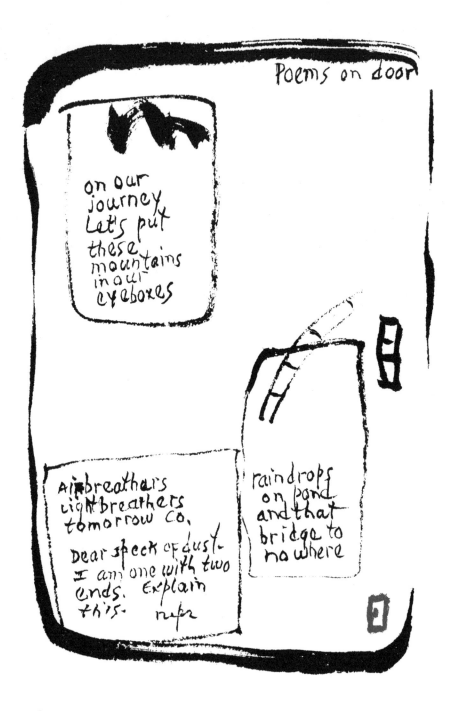

Poems on door

on our
journey
Let's put
these
mountains
in our
eyeboxes

Airbreathers
Lightbreathers
tomorrow Co.

Dear speck of dust—
I am one with two
ends. Explain
this.

raindrops
on pond
and that
bridge to
nowhere

DOOR

A large door.
Cat walks up to it, sniffs, walks away.
Dog comes, pisses on it.
Frail woman approaches, hesitates, goes away.
A business man taps efficiently on the door, then leaves.
A boy bounces a ball against the door, stops.
A rough man comes, pounds on the door: Open up.

The door slowly opens.

MAN: Ah, it's magnetic. *He enters.* Only an empty room.
    He steps outside.

The door slowly closes.

Man, annoyed, pounds again on door: Open, I say.
Pounds and waves arms: Open!
Kicks door: Open or I'll break in.

The door remains closed.

Man gives up,
Sits outside.

The door opens.

The man watches.

A bird flies in.
A bat flies out.
Bird flies out.
Bat flies in.
Cat walks in and out.
Dog pisses on the same place.
A boy and girl sneak in the room,
Close the door.

After a while
A pounding from within: Help! Let me out.

The man laughs, then
As the cries continue
Goes to door and pounds
With the pounding from within:

    Open, I say!

    Help! Let us out.

UNWRINKLING

Girl in room.
Knock on door.
Girl goes to door.
Quiet young man, a Chinese: Good morning, may I sit
    with you?
Girl puzzled: Come in.
Young man enters,
Sits.
Girl sits.
GIRL: Well, what's about?
Young man sits buoyant,
Wordless.
After some time he rises, walks to door,
Bows
And leaves.

Girl, standing,
Goes to mirror, wonders,
Returns to chair,
Sits.

SEED

SEED:

Let's

be

a

tree.

TREE:

Let's

be

a

seed.

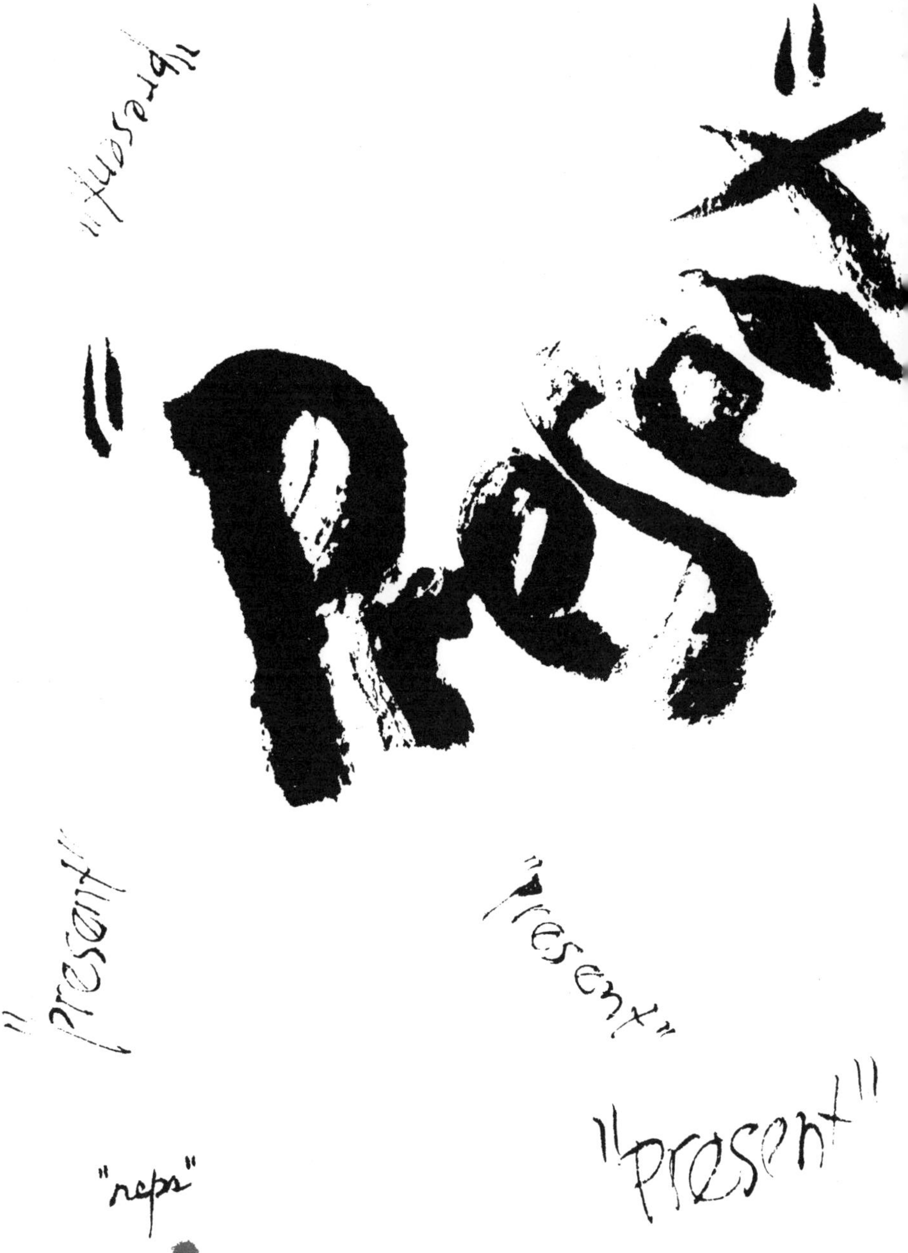
"Present"
"present"
"present"
"present"
"present"
"reps"

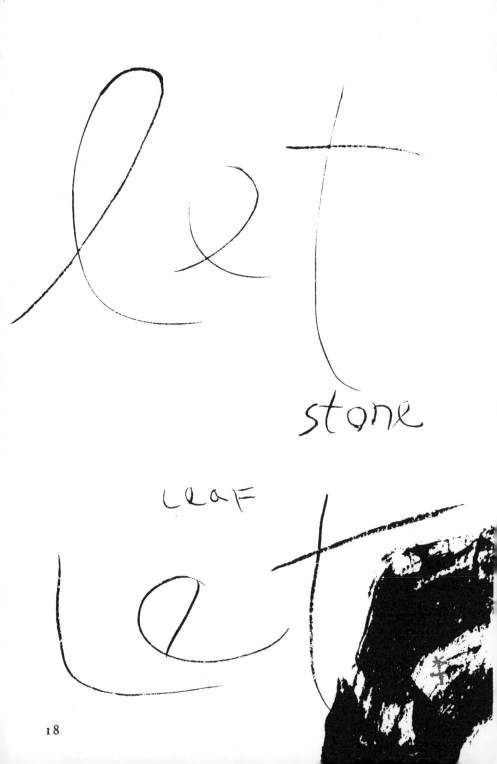

let
stone
LeaF
let

THE BIG WELLING

"Hello. Will you give me some information?"

"Will try."

"In, out of mind, we experience this and that.
Tell me, could there be a big welling
including ordinary experience—
as if unexpected, effortless,
as if seeing many things at once invisibly,
as if watching a play unmoved in moving?"

"Could be."

"An immense refreshing? How does even a little
freshening come?"

"Before   .   moving   .

         let

           .

 any   stir

           .

 start   through."

"O thank you
                    and might it
        in dark
                or
                        turning?

"Might."

                "In fragrancing,
                rain
                spat

                        snow

                    fall

    bird   cry

                or

            placing   branch
                with
                        others

pouring
cup   in
                            glance,

                        with
                        step
                                through
                                feet

                                head
                                hand,

                welling
                    includingly—
                                        in it
                                            the
                                        galaxy

                                            the
                                            dust

                                            feet

                                            touch—"

        "Much."

TURN

SEAMSTRESS *(fitting a dress on a woman)*: Turn please.
  Woman turns.
SEAMSTRESS: Turn.
  Woman turns.
SEAMSTRESS: Shall we decorate, necktie and high heel it?
  Why not turn within too?

WOMAN: I hate you.
SEAMSTRESS: Excuse me, beautiful.

  Woman tears off dress and walks naked
  From the room.
WOMAN *(returning)*: I saw in the mirror, I have nothing
  on.
SEAMSTRESS: Did you turn?

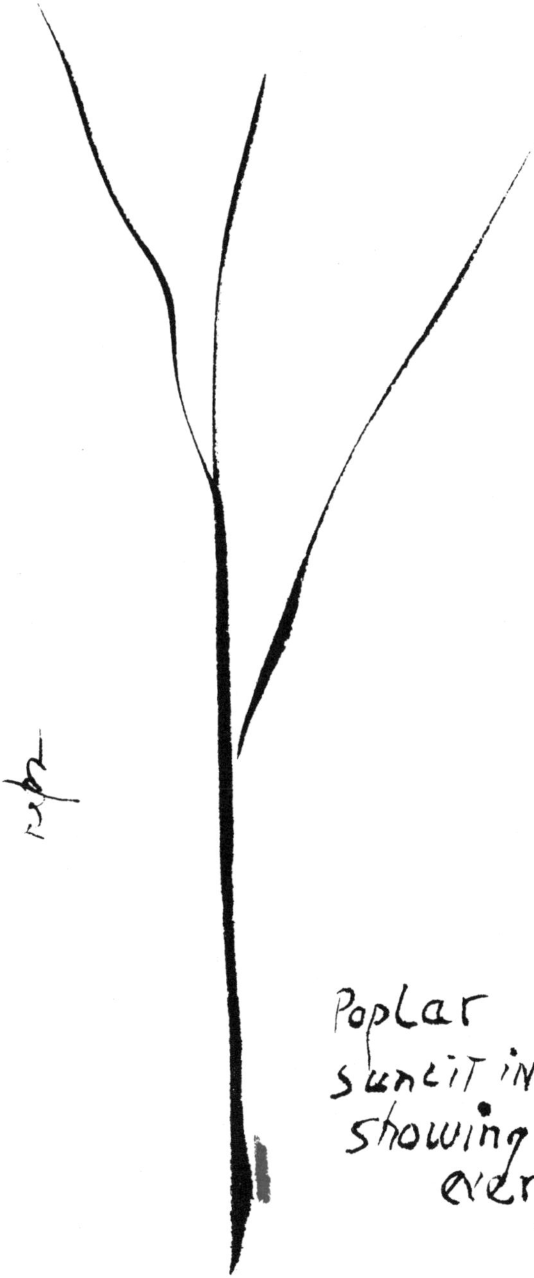

Poplar
sunlit in spring
showing
everything

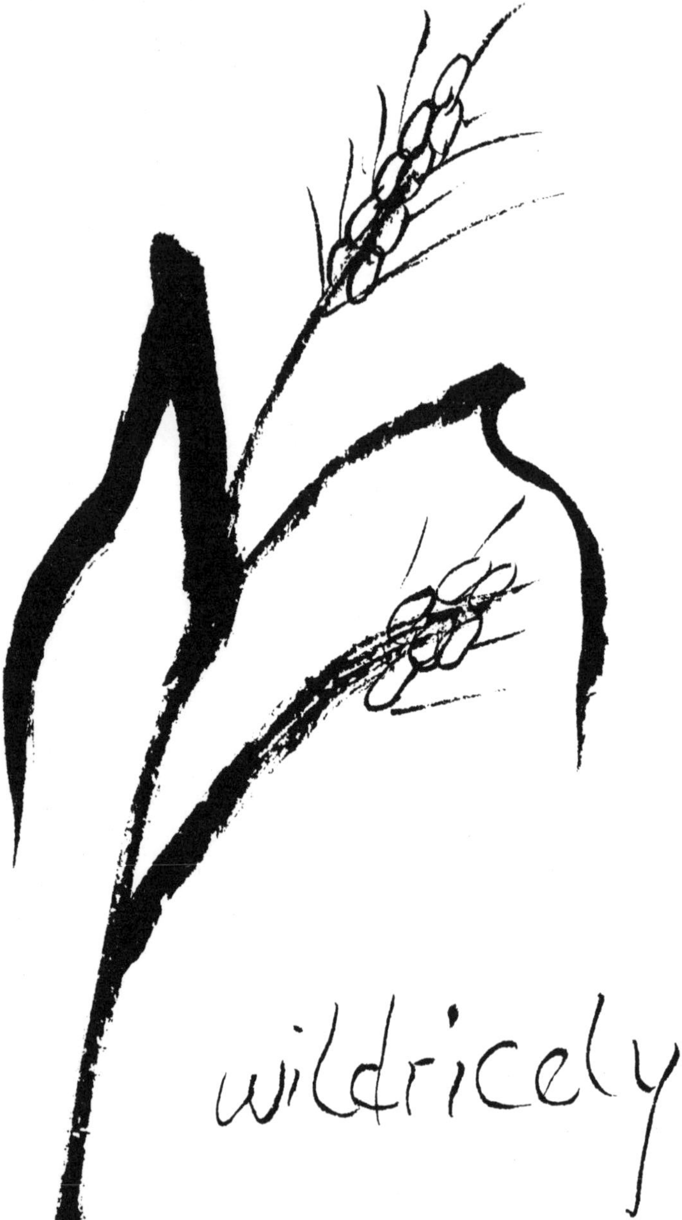
wildricely

GREAT WAVES, SMALL WAVES

Woman walking on her hands
While giving birth to a child.

CHILD: Where am I?

WOMAN: Dear child, you are being born here.

CHILD: Let me out.

WOMAN: Let yourself out.

VILLAGERS

Earth has become a village of many colors.

NEGRO: Night breathes us out, day breathes us in.

AMERICAN: I don't know about that. We make machines to make machines to fill any man's need.

CHINESE: And overfill. We need emptying along with things.

INDIAN: We need God, India always has said and searched.

MOSLEM: Our need is Allah, presently.

ESKIMO: What are these strange names? Haven't we eyes to see, ears to hear the silent word?

NEGRO: We hear.

CHINESE: The word is us.

INDIAN: Let us chant it together in our night-day dream.

MOSLEM: Agreed.

ESKIMO: With bear, seal, porpoise, penguin.

AMERICAN: Friend, you would go backward, we to world constructs.

INDIAN: We have gone to many worlds and without machines.

MOSLEM: Worlds, worlds, specks in Allah's eye, sighs in his sigh.

CHINESE: We are villagers, remember this.

JAPANESE: Bamboo rustles
    without wind.

NEGRO: May I sing the aliving word for you?

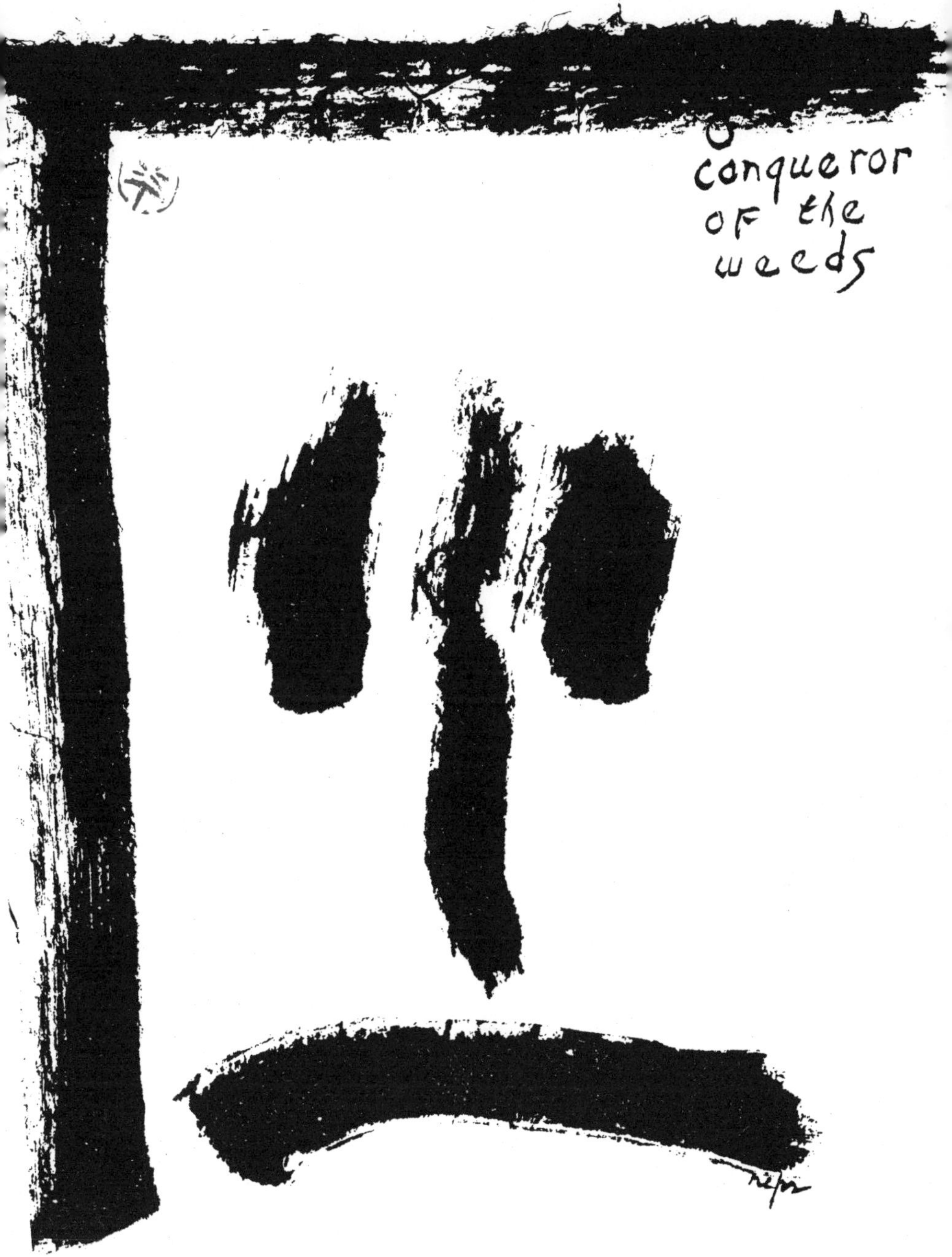
O
conqueror
of the
weeds

GOAT LIFE

SHEEP *(going to market, to a goat)*: What will become of
 me?

GOAT *(going to market)*: They will eat you.

SHEEP: I want to eat, not to be eaten. Will they eat you
 too?

GOAT: They will, but I shall pierce them with my horns.
 The scene changes to one foul and bloody.

MAN: Come here, sheep. No one lives forever. *(Slits its
 throat.)*

SHEEP *(to goat)*: Pierce them!

GOAT *(as its throat is slit)*: Death eater, eat my death.

The sheep who is no longer a sheep awakes.
The goat who is no longer a goat awakes.
The man who is no longer a man awakes.

SHEEP: It was a dream.

GOAT: A horror.

MAN: Forgive me.

SHEEP: You are forgiven.

GOAT: What is there to forgive in a nightmare?

MAN: Forgive me in the nightmare.

GOAT: Forget it.

MAN: I can't.

SHEEP: Since, again, you shall be sheep and I a man who
 slits your throat. And goat, what shall you be?

GOAT: Waking from a bad dream why go back into it?
 Let's be what passes all imagination.

SHEEP: A man who loves?

MAN: Some yet greater being?

GOAT: You two are still dreaming. You have wool and
 knife in mind. Shall we be what we always have
 been, always will be?

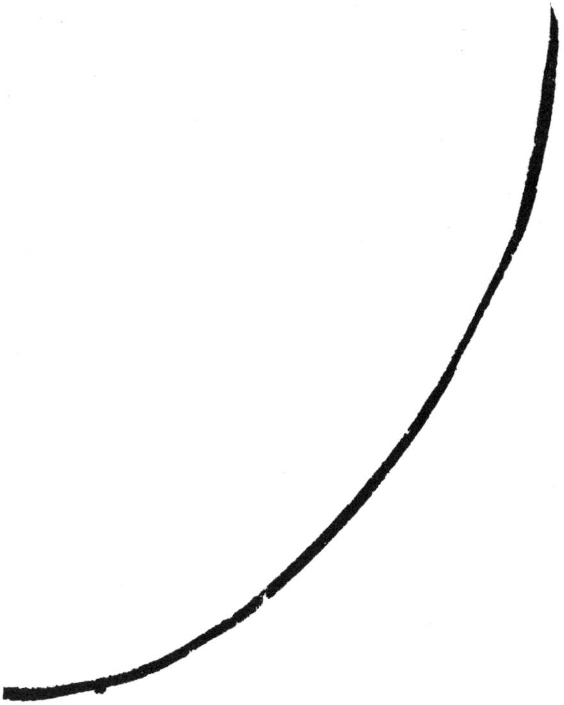

Why
the rush
there's a
moon
For everyone

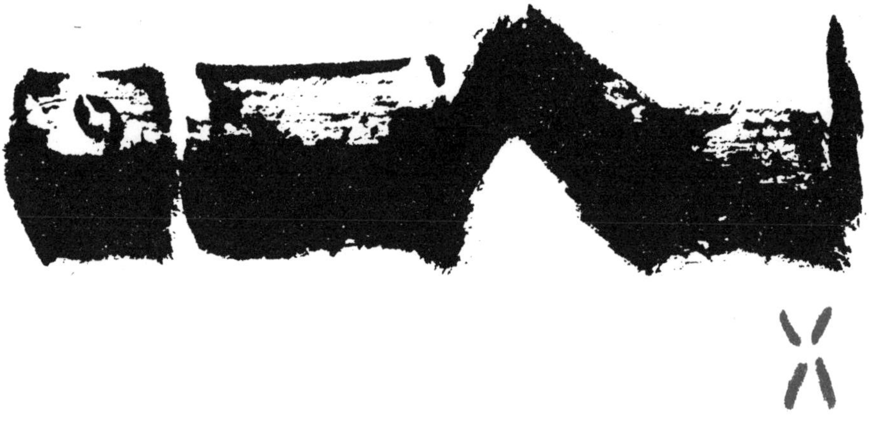

UPSTREAMING

This play is produced in less than a week.

A river. Summer.
A man stands waist-high in the water, facing upstream.
He stands there all day
Indrinking earth and air.
He is there the next day.
Villagers notice him.
A young woman ventures to bring him some brown rice.
He accepts it without changing postion.

Others join him.
Some philosophers come to confer on the bank without
Entering the water.
Scientists take the river's temperature and
Decide the man exemplifies some profound truth
Or other. They name it upstreaming.

News of this spreads.
People come from far away to stand in the river.
They enjoy it.
No one talks,
The water is cool,
The wind like wine.
It is good to be barefoot
And to look into sky.

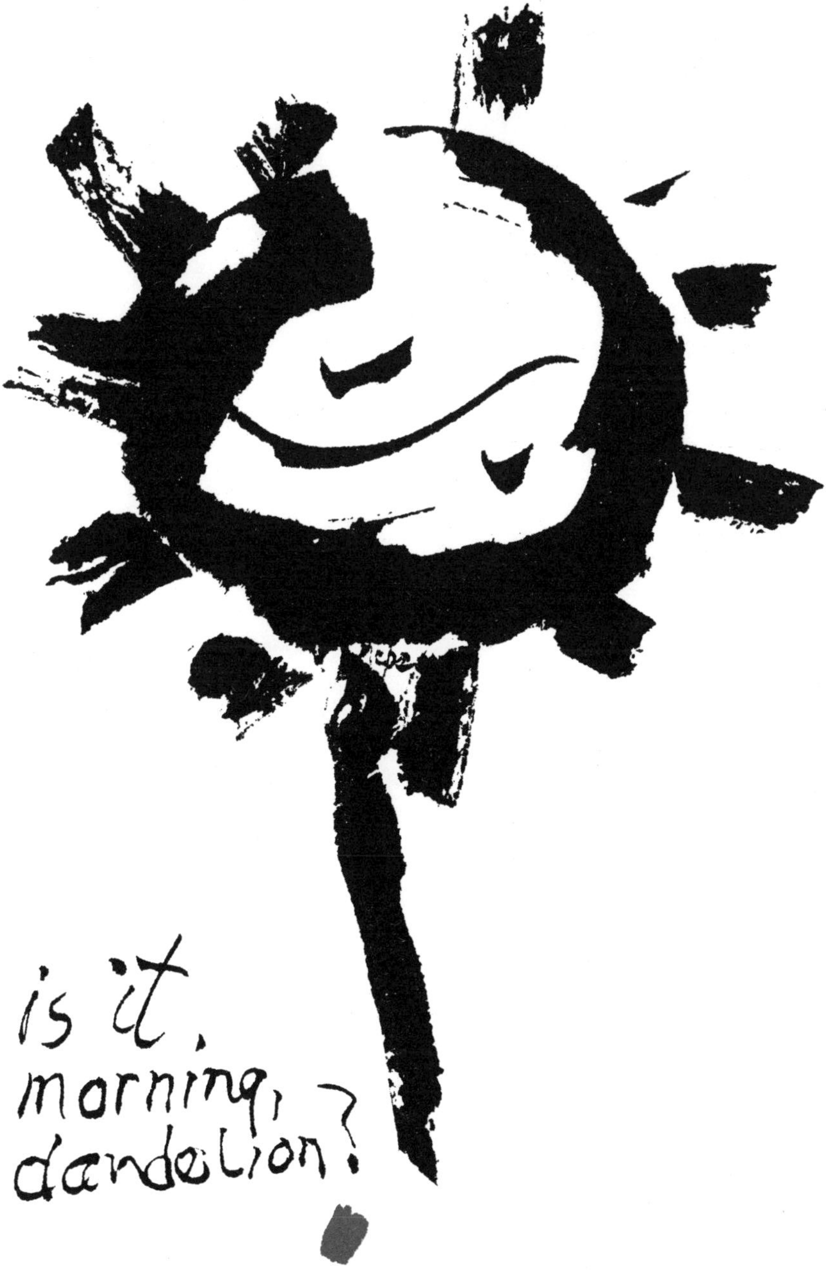
is it,
morning,
dandelion?

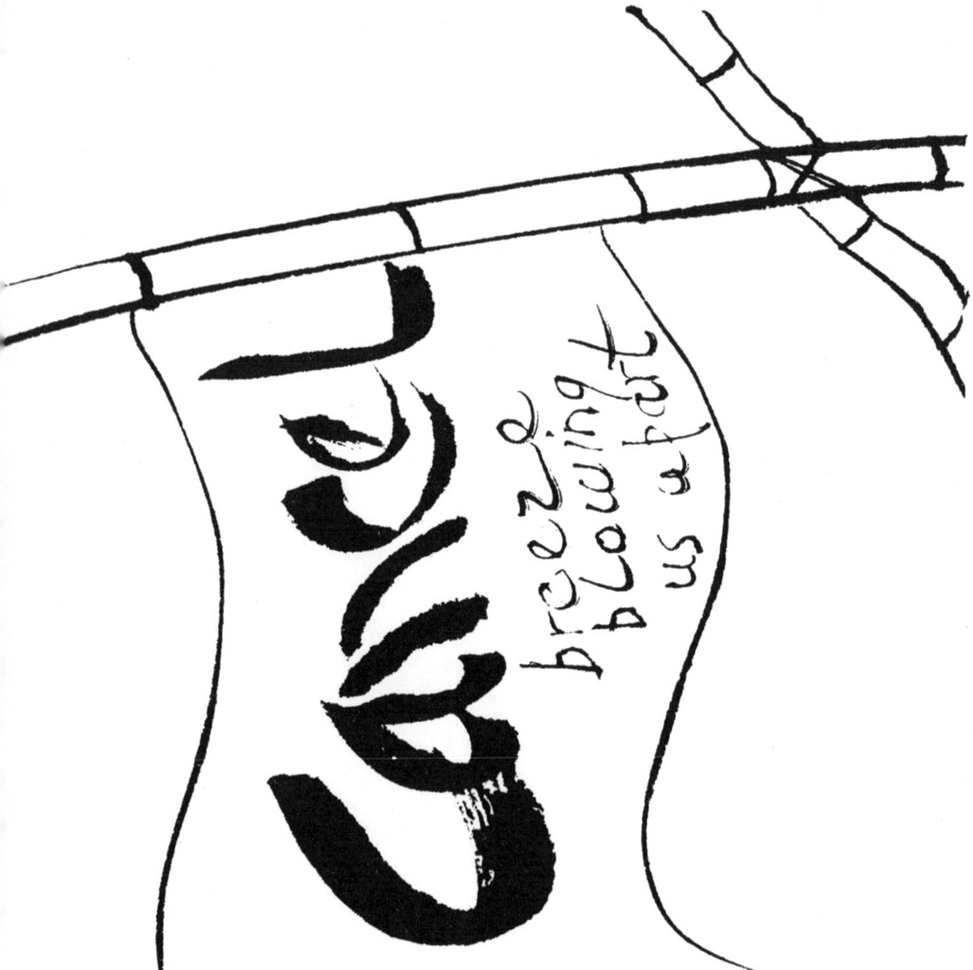
breeze
blowing
us apart

LESS THAN MORE

Outside an airport in Japan.
The players:

> HU-MAN *in Buddhist monk robes, carrying three nine-inch square wood boxes*
> More-than-Human
> Less-than-More

HU-MAN: Dear Less, come here.

LESS: Here I am, your servant, friend, enemy, whatever you wish.

HU-MAN: Carry these boxes for a while.

LESS: Are you tired? It was your idea.

HU-MAN: Of course, everything's my idea—that I'm a Buddhist monk, that my teacher died whose ashes are in this box, and his teacher before him in this box, and his teacher's teacher.

LESS: But they are only three and teachers go back to more than 30, 300, 3,000 to the beginning of parents and teachers.

HU-MAN: We are carrying all of them in our cells.

LESS: What place did they like best in your round-the-world trip? Egypt? India? China? Or just flying?

HU-MAN: You know living and dead intermingle.

LESS: And all else. Would you like a woman?

HU-MAN: Less, I never understand you. Don't ask such things.

LESS: You are thinking of your mother again. Mother, sweetheart, daughter—all women are the same to me.

HU-MAN *(somewhat distraught)*: More, please appear.

MORE *(who as Less has the power to appear in any form)*: Present.

HU-MAN: Thank you, dear More. Please revive me with your presence, Less too, these boxes too.

MORE: It is done.

Hu-man and Less become livelier.

HU-MAN: What a glorious day!

LESS: Let's go, let's go.

MORE: Take it easy, fellows.

The three start to walk hand in hand,
Hu-man determinedly with Less holding his left hand loosely and carrying the boxes,
More on his right striding as if clearing the atmosphere.
They make way for a girl approaching them. She is weeping.
Less puts down the boxes and lays hands on her but she does not notice it.
Hu-man bows as she passes.
The girl turns and looks back at Hu-man as he turns to look at her.
They all stop.

HU-MAN: Does something trouble you?

GIRL: My parents left the world today.

LESS *(to Hu-man)*: Would you carry them too?

HU-MAN *(to girl)*: I am sorry.

MORE: You are sorry? Tell her truth.

HU-MAN: In the world of the dead there is death but not in the world of the living.

GIRL: Tell me about the living world.

MORE: Tell her.

HU-MAN: I can't. I'm still in the dead world. You tell her.

MORE: She doesn't notice me.

LESS: Tell her of my world, of under and green and grow, of rooting, of spiraling.

GIRL: Tell me everything.

HU-MAN: How shall I tell you? A woman knows more than a man, much more than a monk.

MORE: He shall tell you through some person you see, somewhere you be.

GIRL: Be? Be?

Hu-man picks up the boxes and starts on,
His steps in quickening yeses as
More and Less go in the other direction with the girl.

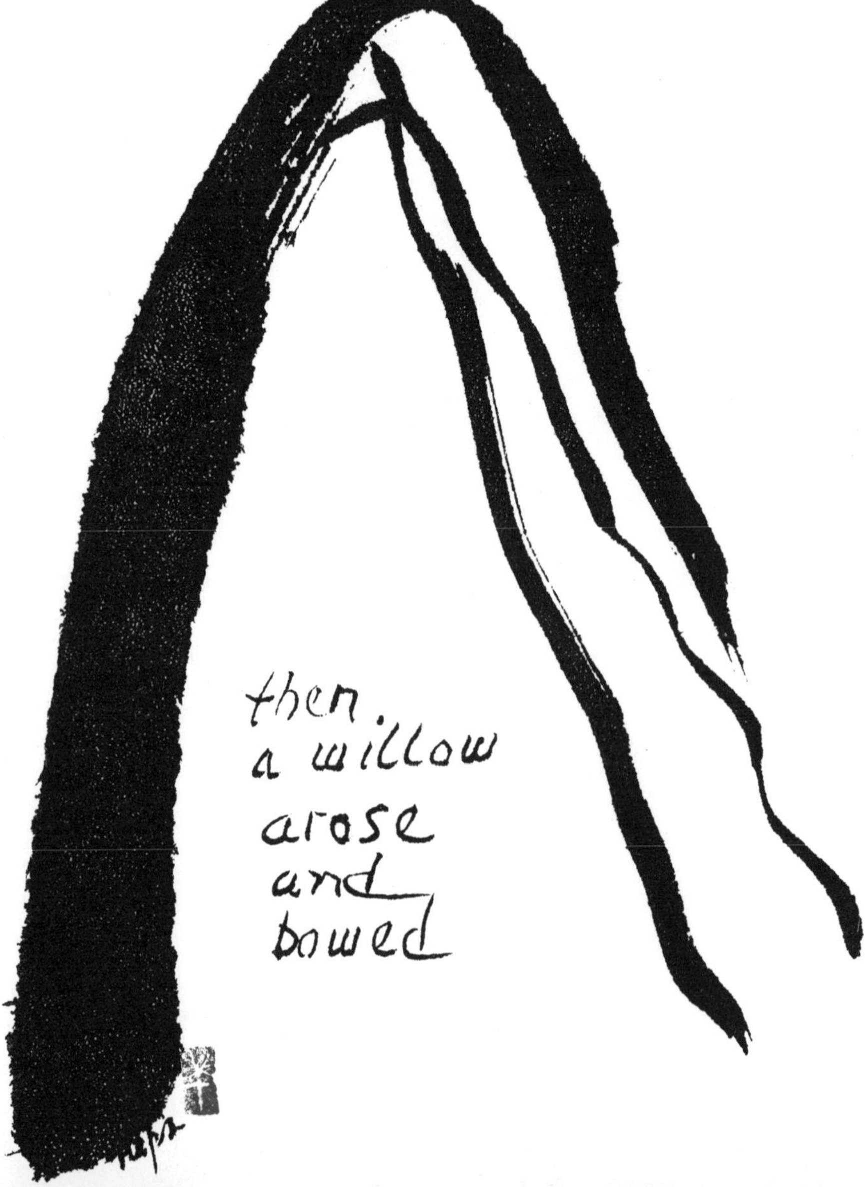
then
a willow
arose
and
bowed

AS IF

mathematics of bee:
"1"
"2"
"3"
"in-finity"

or way of worm

or bliss
of
bird

or
compose
of
cat

or but
of butterfly

or
dear
of
deer

or
man, the only creature who works, asks,
"Can they all be wrong but me?"

A bamboo grove in a rice field.
Two statues, a Buddha and a Jesus.

SOMEONE:

And   when
          most   comfortable
                    and   when
    asleep
            and   at

                              unexpected

              times
        our mind, our attention

    goes
    into
    heart

                              warmer
                              stronger

    here

    we

    are.

BAMBOO: Are? did someone say?

MANGO TREE *(dropping a mango):* Plop.

BAMBOO: It's a seed I hear.

WIND *(disturbing Bamboo's balance):* Whoo.

RICE PLANT: Accept us, soil,
    accept us, sun.

CLOUD: No trouble at all.

ROCKS: Are
  are.

BUDDHA STATUE: Someone locked me in here.

TWIG: Twig.

JESUS STATUE: They did it to me too.

ROCK: Wait   .

       ten   .

     twenty.

        million .

    years.

       until .

     tears.

WORM: Patience, brothers.

MANGO: Plop.

THE UNKILL

In the woods, in the dark, a small clearing.

The killer lying there. Another man appears, the killed.

KILLER: Get going.

KILLED: In the dark I can't see the color of your skin.

KILLER: I said get going.

KILLED: But I can hear your voice.

Both men attack.

KILLER *(holding knife over the fallen man)*: Die.

KILLED: No.

KILLER *(as his hard fists open)*: Afraid?

KILLED: No. Isn't death life? Isn't it a breath, a play?

KILLER *(plunging knife into killed)*: Die.

KILLED: Haaa!

CROW: Caw.

COW: Moo.

KILLER: *silent.*

CROW: Caw.

COW: Moo.

KILLER: *silent.*

CROW: Caw.

COW: Moo.

KILLER: Boo!

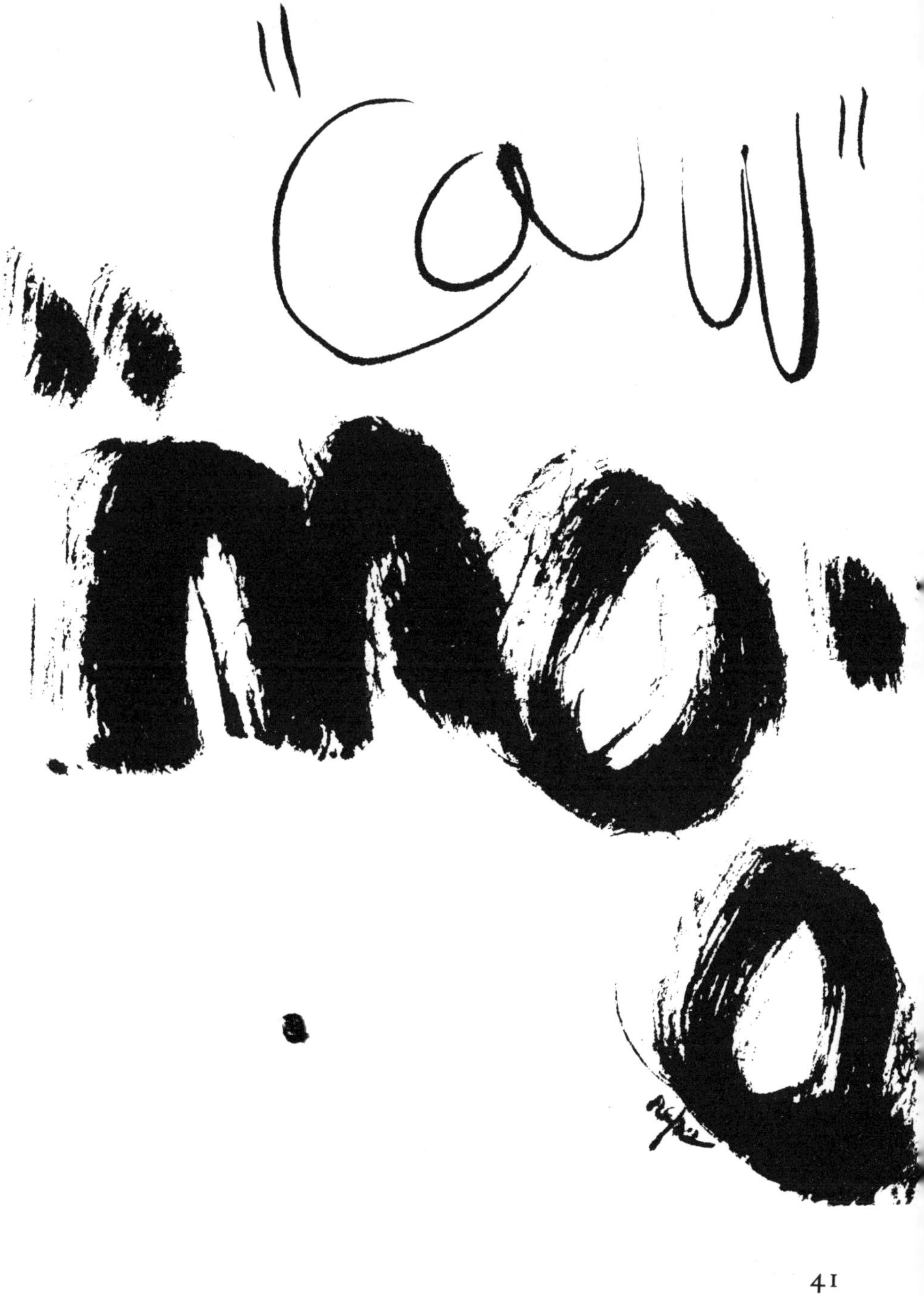
"Call"
moo

SCHOOLROOM

A schoolroom.

Music from somewhere.

TEACHER *(to a former pupil walking by)*: Come in, come in. Would you pass by and not say hello to your old teacher?

PUPIL: Hello. I have thanked and do thank you. But I have another teacher now.

TEACHER: Of course. What are you studying after all these years, chemistry, mathematics, biology?

PUPIL: The possible world within us.

TEACHER: Anatomy?

PUPIL: My teacher gives us our instrument and a word.

TEACHER: A word?

PUPIL: I am to sit quietly, receiving some word.

TEACHER *(astonished)*: What?

PUPIL: We let breath breathe—until it is all love breathing. Then we silently feel some word as breath flows down and up.

TEACHER: Then what do you do?

PUPIL: Do? The great breath enters my being.

TEACHER *(walking about, considering)*: Surely a silent singing could do us no harm.

Fern and fawn have theirs.

Bear hibernates with slower breaths and longer pauses.

Turtle has an inner melody.

Some name this faith, some prayer.

To you it is the good breath.

PUPIL: Why don't you teach it?

TEACHER: Perhaps I may.

A transparent room.

A hundred thousand pupils.

The teacher.

Music from somewhere.

19 poems

Birch
mists

    Listen
    IN
  green stem

streaming
shimmering
stones

    thistles
    clouds
    would be

Tree
trying to be
tree

   Frog
   stone-brown

over
roots
under

mushroom
soft loam
home

in it
in it
bird
chirps

    and
    bamboo

red berries
without seeing
    see

rippling

spider skynet
nobody
here

warm
wings
sing

drops
after rain

dance
stems
dance

something

never

    Leafs

suns
in
sand

tip

of

reed

reʃɔ

POISON

Two clouds pass through two clouds.
An artificial flower looks at a flower
And says let us be married. It is still.
But what is it? Suddenly—faint bird calls.
They destroyed our woodlands.
They ravished the meadows.
They shot us in air.
Taking yellow leaves for gold, red for blood,
    never seeing their faces in the broken ones.
They could not sing, so they poisoned us.
Kill, kill, kill must be their will.
When their moment comes they may not even enter
    insects for they only believe in death.
Because they could not fly.
Because they would not sing.

we pass
outvoted
by the grass

reps

DANCING KEYS

Coffee percolating glumb glug flug.
A child moves with its sounds.

Old washing machine
Clankety kong ung clankety.
Mother moves with its sounds.

Man enters,
Sees mother and child closed-eyed moving in,
Joins them
In rhythm of percolater, washing machine,
Insects, reeds, roots,

silent in sound.

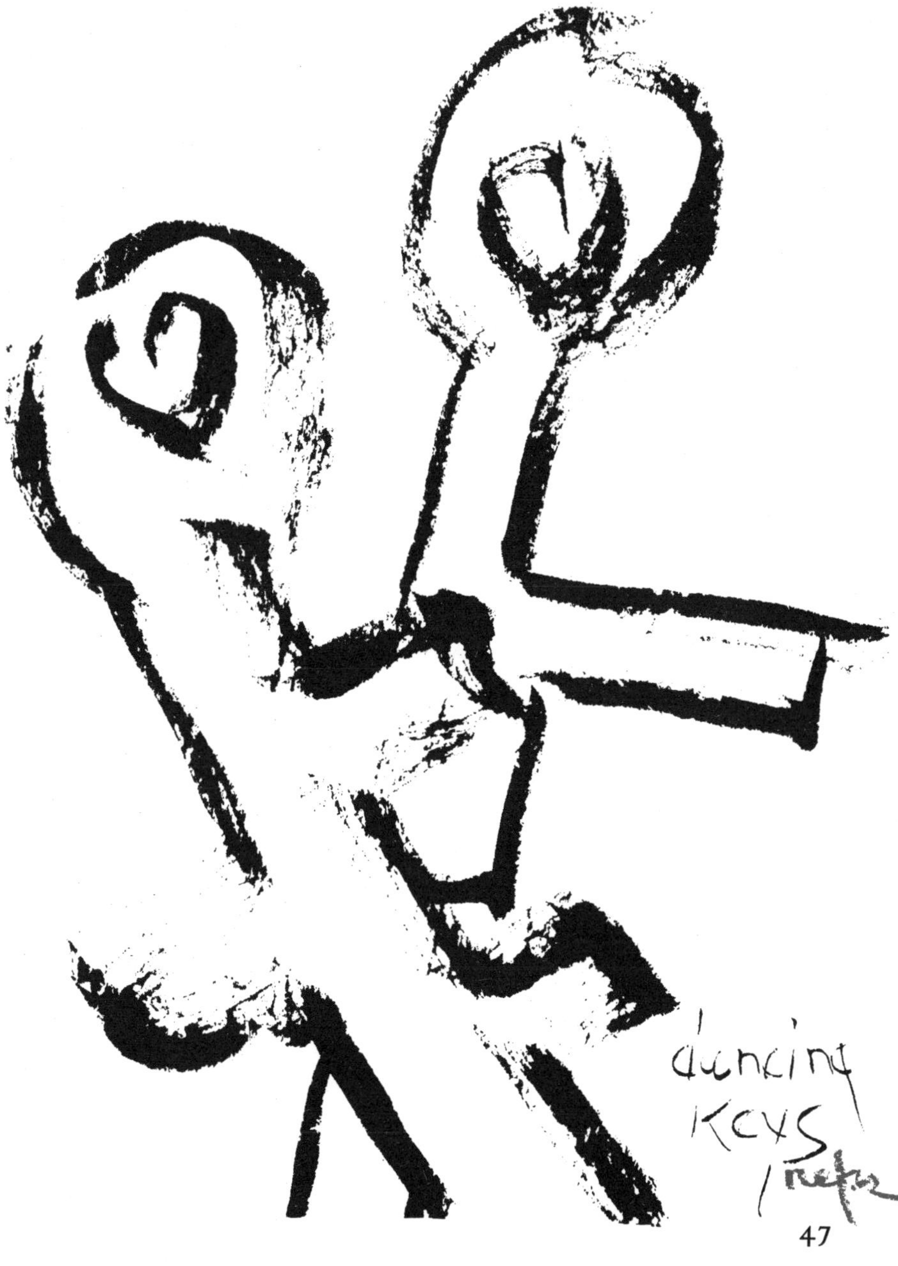
dancing
keys

BOXED

1ST BOX: I am box, his private box.
2ND BOX: I'm hers.
3D BOX: I'm its. They stuff me with their things.

1ST BOX: He he's.
2ND BOX: She she's.
3D BOX: I only it, not hot, not cold.

1ST BOX: Why must our owners sleep in us. Gypsies
  sleep outdoors.
2ND BOX: Only sleep. Outside they're free, tossing a
  ball, free.
3D BOX: Yes, when we are free.

1st Box removes one side.

2nd Box removes two sides.

3rd Box removes all sides.

HE *(coming out of dream):* It never happened!
SHE: What ever happened.

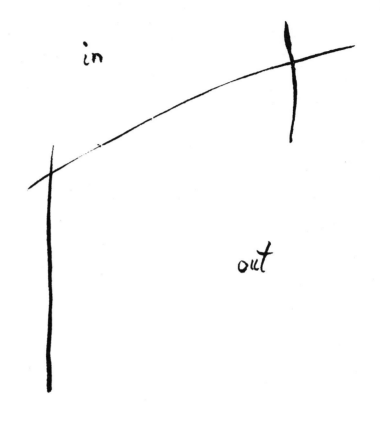

in

out

Free

nepa

ATTACK

The action of the samurai swordsmen is so fast it cannot be seen.

It is shown here in slow motion, described by a speaker.

SPEAKER: Each has one enemy.
    See. White lifts his shining sword and attacks.
    Black diverts the attack with his sword and at the moment its force has almost ebbed he attacks.
    White counters Black's attack.
    At the moment its force has almost ebbed he attacks again with an emptying shout.
    Black channels that.
    White pauses.
    Black pauses.
    Each searches the center of the other's attention.
    It is high noon, midnight.
    It is you, me.
    Do not be alarmed.
    These swordsmen will not turn their weapons on us.
    We too have weapons, we would slice them in two in a flash.
    Do not think I am moralizing. Do not think.
    It is too late.
    Someone seems to have cut me in two.
    Was it *you?*

hush

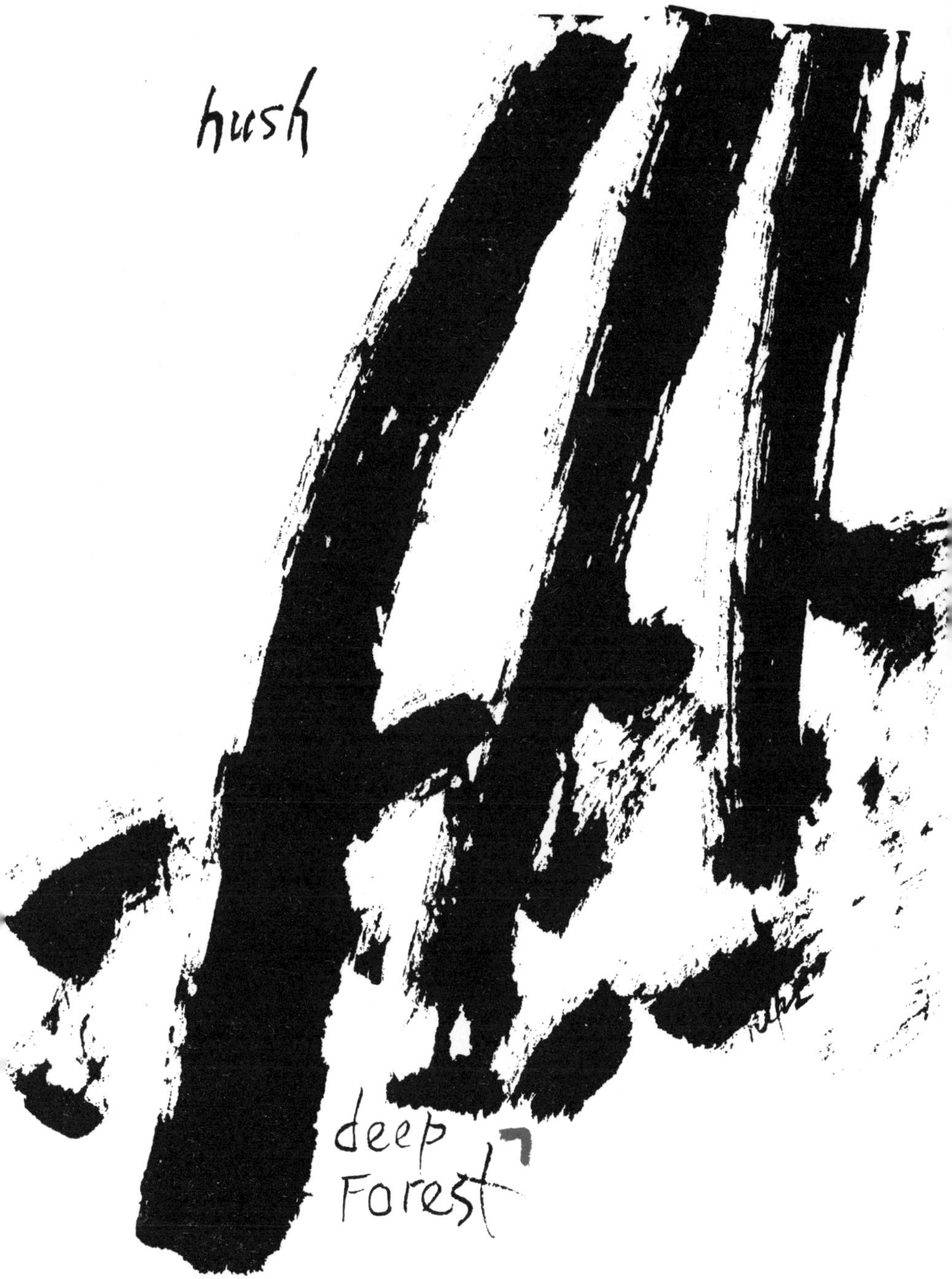

deep
Forest

UNKNOT

"Man, what are you fishing for? You have no
     hook."
"I am guiding the paths of birds."
     "How?"
"Fly here, fly there."
     "You say it afterwards."
"Unknot and see for yourself."
     "Unknot? Is that what you're doing, so still?"
"I don't know—freshly."
     "Man, I don't get you. No hook, no fish, doing
     nobody no good."
"Who does good, the turtle?"
     "I do. I support my wife."
"Is she falling over?"
     "Look, that fish has a paper. It's coming my way.
     What does it say? A song?"
          "Within a whole
               there is a
                    hole
               everything
                    falls
                    into,
               even the worlds,
               even the hole
          that turning inside out
          lo, a hole is all about."

"That's good. A fish brings me a tune.
Well, so long, man. Don't fall into any holes."

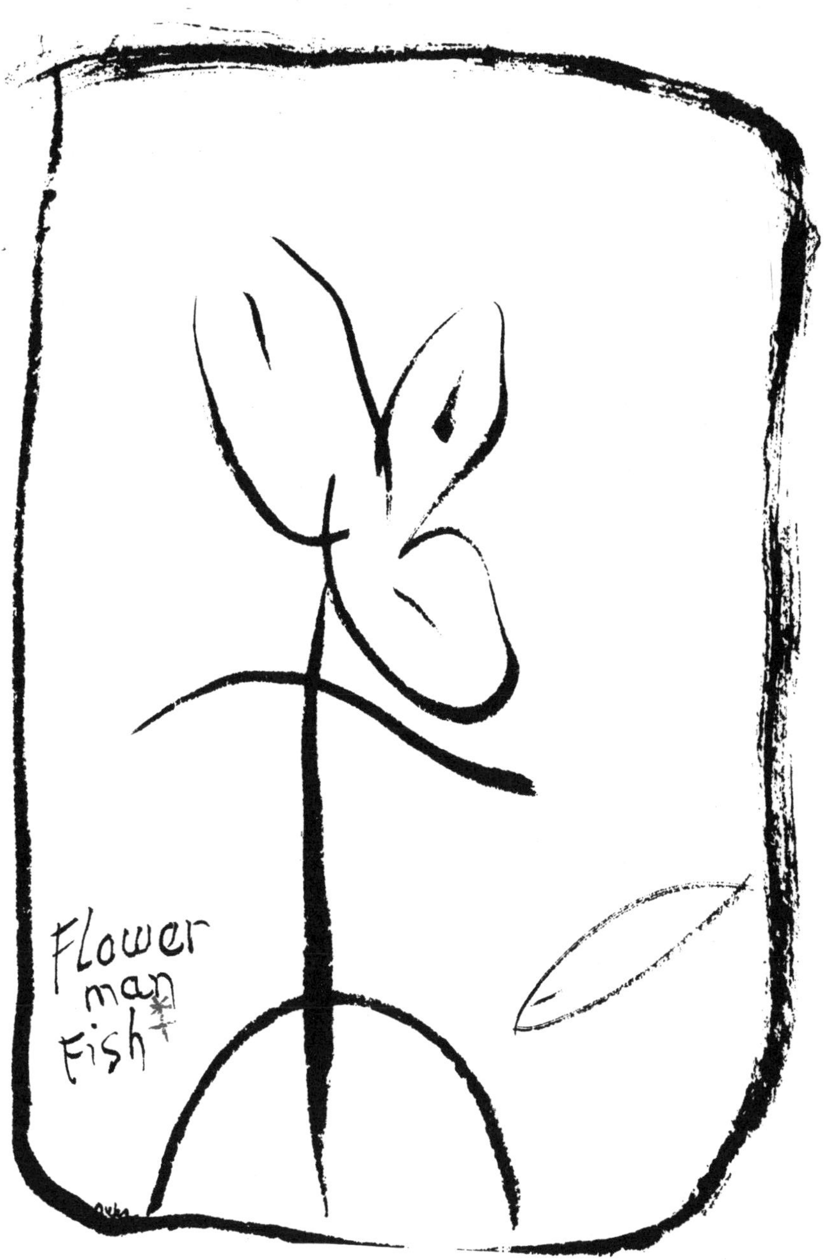
Flower
man
Fish

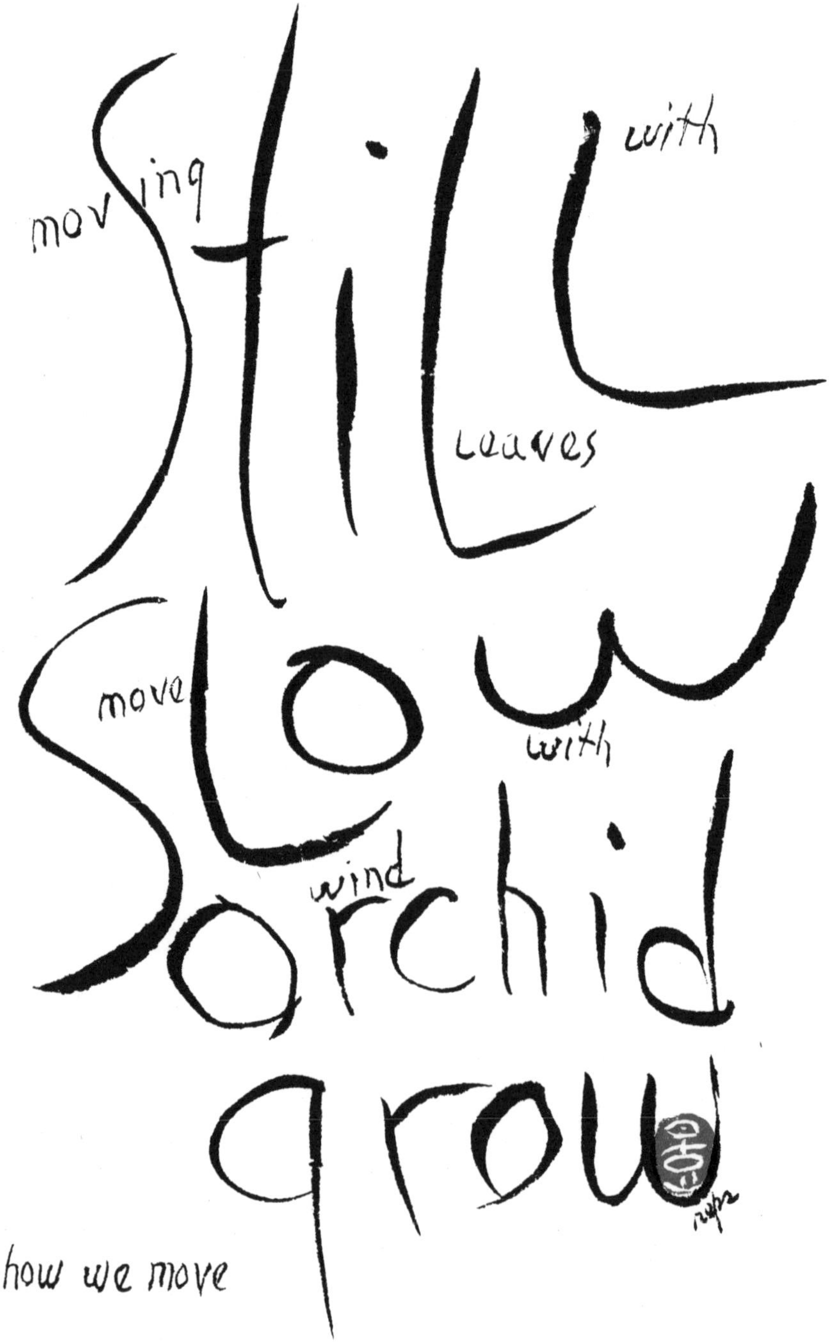
Still
moving
with
leaves
Slow
move
with
wind
orchid
grow
how we move

ACCORDINGLY

3,000 musicians of the world assembled in a vast gossamer dome.

CHAIRMAN: We will now hear the music of Lucia Dlugoszewski.

Half the audience leaves.

SOMEONE: Mr Chairman, I protest this disrespectful departure.

VOICE: We didn't come here to hear a nobody.

ANOTHER: Did you say it's a woman?

Half of those remaining leave.

SOMEONE: Mr Chairman, it has been said she is the best woman composer and that she makes her own instruments.

Half again walk out.

SOMEONE: Mr Chairman, she can't play here.

CHAIRMAN: Why not?

THE SOMEONE: We would lose our jobs.

More straggle out.

VOICE: Why would we lose our jobs?

THE SOMEONE: Because after hearing her we'd be imitators, that's why. She's infectious.

VOICE: That's absurd.

THE SOMEONE: It isn't absurd. Her music touches those hearing it with a carefree ecstacy, and then they won't go for the old stuff. It isn't music to them any more.

OTHERS: Let's hear her anyway.

CHAIRMAN: Meeting come to order, what's left of it. We are now adjourned for later consideration.

Chairman leaves.
A thin girl enters and arranges 101 newly invented in-instruments of skin, wool, wood, metal, glass, paper.
There are ladder harps, tangent and unsheltered rattles,
Wind bells, gongs,
Drums for claws and fingers.

She begins to play.
It is she.
It is and it isn't music
Penetrating clarities
Delicate variances
Accidental and tiny distractions
Radiances
Suchness of sounds
Undulations
Like no music ever heard before
Tingles
Tangles
Untangles
Spontaneates
Pounces
Burrows
Bewilders
Laughs
Like music of winds
Garden-growing sounds
Children at play
Like the music of other worlds?
Like happy
Sprinkles
Those listening begin to hear
Become rocks giraffes tumbleweeds
Embrace
Sway with eyes closed
Move on out of the dome
With never the same melody
Wherever they go
Others join them
Others join the joiners
More and more
A new kind of music
New kind of world.

For a small poem show:
.   take poems from book and scotch-tape
      from top to cord-tied bamboo poles
      or to clotheslines like washing.

.   Let the wind blow.

.   Look.

Poem shows:

Japan, Kyoto	Sankakudo	1957
Japan, Osaka	Takashimaya	1957
Japan, Tokyo	Takashimaya	1958
Japan, Kyoto	Marubutsu	1958
Japan, Kyoto	Omsha	1959
USA, Texas	San Angelo Gallery	1960
New Zealand	Colleges	1960
USA, California	Pomona College	1961
USA, California	San Francisco	
	Batman Gallery	1962
USA, California	Chico	1963
JAPAN, Tokyo	Ohsawa	1963
USA, California	Big Spur	1964